MIX IT UP

Simple and Customizable Recipes for the Young and the Young at Heart

Megan Byrkit

ACKNOWLEDGEMENTS:

My dream of writing a cookbook would not have come true without the people who supported me along the way. My mom and dad always assisted me even though I spent hours taking over their kitchen, and were so gracious to me as I tested each recipe again and again. Not only did my parents support me as I wrote this book, but they also had a great impact on my passion for baking. Growing up I have such fond memories making Sunday morning waffles with my dad and making cookies with my mom. Finally, I could never leave out my fabulous taste testers, my siblings, Mac and Grace. They always encouraged me and helped me finish off each treat!

DEDICATION:

I dedicate this cookbook to my mom and dad, who have supported me throughout my entire baking adventure!

ABOUT THE AUTHOR:

Megan Byrkit is a 15-year-old with a passion for creative cooking. She loves to mix up ordinary recipes by using her own special ingredient: imagination. When Megan isn't mixing away in her family's kitchen, she enjoys spending time with friends, dancing, and watching sunsets. Megan's first cookbook, Mix It Up, was inspired by her belief that baking is not just about following rules but a process of experimenting to create delicious memories. She hopes to inspire people of all ages to dive into the kitchen and add their own special touch to each recipe.

CONTENTS:

HELPFUL KITCHEN TIPS

Measuring:

    Tablespoon = Tbsp

    Teaspoon = tsp

1 Tbsp = 3 tsp

¼ cup = 4 Tbsp

⅓ cup = 5 Tbsp+1 tsp

1 cup = 16 Tbsp

½ cup = 1 stick of butter

When measuring dry ingredients use a knife to level off excess on the top of a measuring cup. For wet ingredients, set your measuring tool on a flat surface.

Before measuring sticky ingredients, run your measuring tool under hot water and quickly dry it with a towel.

Substitutes:

1 tsp Cream of tartar: 1 tsp Lemon Juice

1 Tbsp Maple Syrup: 1 Tbsp Honey

1 Tbsp Margarine or Coconut Oil: 1 Tbsp Butter

1 tsp Baking Soda: 3 tsp baking powder

Oat flour: Blend oats in a blender/food processor until smooth

Powdered sugar/confectioners sugar: For 1 cup, blend 1 cup of granulated sugar in a food processor/blender with 1 tsp cornstarch until powdery.

Gluten free:

Use a 1:1 gluten free flour substitute. I recommend Bob's Red mill and King Arthur's gluten free flour. I have tested these recipes using gluten free flour and they will still turn out great!

Dairy free:

Several recipes are not labeled dairy free because of chocolate chips, so use a dairy free chocolate chip and you're good to go! Otherwise, use dairy free milk or butter substitutes.

Recommended Kitchen Tools:

Silicone mats: to cover/grease baking sheets, if you do not have one, use butter or baking spray.

Cookie scoop: spring loaded scoop, to ensure proportionate sizes, and it quickly forms dough into a dome. Use a spoon, or even an ice cream scoop, if not.

Cooling Racks- wire racks to place your fresh baked good on, so it cools quickly and evenly.

Sifter- removes any large unwanted pieces. If you do not have a sifter and are instructed to sift in a recipe, pulse the ingredient in a food processor instead.

Electric Mixer- high speed mixing tool is used in almost every baking recipe, you can use either a hand-held mixer, or a stand mixer.

How-To's and Common Q's:

Soften/Melt/Brown Butter: Pop your butter in a microwave-safe bowl on low power for a few seconds to soften it. To completely melt butter, heat it over the stove in a small pot, or put it in the microwave on high power for 10-20 seconds until fully melted. To brown butter, heat it in a small pot over the stove until small brown specks appear.

Melt Chocolate: Whether you melt your chocolate in a microwave safe bowl or even the stove, make sure to add a little bit of oil. For 1 cup chocolate I use 1 tsp oil.

Whip Egg Whites: Use an electric mixer on high speed for several minutes. Your eggs will go through several stages, foamy and soft peaks, until they finally reach stiff peaks, so do not give up. You have reached the "stiff peak stage" when the egg whites stand up straight if you lift up your mixer. Wipe down your bowl, to remove any oil before whipping egg whites, and make sure to not have any egg yolk, as any fat left with the egg whites will make it difficult to whip into stiff peaks.

Room-Temperature Eggs: For some pastries and desserts, if specified, it is important to use room-temperature eggs. Rather than waiting 30 minutes, you can warm up eggs quickly By setting them in a bowl under warm running water for 2 minutes.

Is It Done?: It can be difficult to know when baked goods are not over/under-baked. I recommend setting a timer for the lower-end of the baking time, because you can always bake a little more, but once it is burnt, it's burnt! One helpful trick is to poke your baked goods with a toothpick when you think it is done baking, if the toothpick comes out clean (no batter) it's ready!

Salted or Unsalted Butter: Really just a preference! all of my recipes will work with both.

Cooling dough: In some recipes I recommend chilling dough in the fridge for a period of time before baking for a chewier cookie, but it is not required, if you're in a pinch.

Cornstarch: I also often recommend cornstarch in recipes as a special ingredient to enhance texture, but if you don't have it, you do not have to include it.

Cupcake ratings: A difficulty scale, 1 cupcake: easy, 2: medium, 3: hard

Difficulty: 🧁
Yields: 12 cookies
Gluten Free, Dairy Free

Ingredients:

- ¾ cup granulated sugar
- 1 egg
- 1 cup peanut butter

3 INGREDIENT PEANUT BUTTER COOKIES

Directions:

1. Preheat the oven to 325° and line grease a baking sheet.
2. Whisk the eggs and sugar.
3. Stir in peanut butter.
4. Poll into balls and place on a baking sheet.
5. Gently press balls to flatten them slightly.
6. Bake for 10 minutes, and allow time for them to cool.

Mix It Up:

For Thumbprint cookies, use your thumb to make a small imprint on the cookies right after they are removed from the oven. Fill this small hole with jam or a hershey kiss!

Difficulty: 🧁
Yields: 12 Cookies
Gluten Free

Ingredients:

- 3 ripe bananas
- 2 cups oats
- ⅓ cup chocolate chips
- ¼ cup brown sugar

BANANA BREAKFAST COOKIES

Directions:

1. Preheat the oven to 350° and line or grease a baking sheet.
2. Mash bananas with a fork, until smooth, it is okay if it appears chunky.
3. Stir oats, brown sugar, and chocolate chips.
4. Use your hands to roll dough into 12 balls and place on a baking sheet.
5. Bake for 10-15 minutes, or until golden.
6. Allow them to cool for 10 minutes to firm up, or enjoy them hot, gooey, and fresh!

Mix It Up:

Try adding your own mix-ins, such as nuts or a little bit of peanut butter! For more flavor, add some vanilla extract.

Difficulty: 🧁🧁
Yields: 12-14 Cookies

Ingredients:

- 1 cup packed brown sugar
- ¼ cup granulated sugar
- 1 egg
- ½ cup melted butter
- 1 ½ tsp vanilla extract
- 1 ¼ cup flour
- ½ tsp baking soda
- 1 tsp baking powder
- ¼ tsp salt
- 2 tsp cornstarch
- 1 cup chocolate chips/ other add-ins

BIG CHEWY CHOCOLATE CHIP COOKIES

Directions:

1. Preheat the oven to 325°. Line or grease 2 baking sheets.
2. In a small bowl, whisk flour, baking soda, baking powder, salt, and cornstarch
3. In a large bowl whisk melted butter, brown sugar, and white sugar. Add egg and vanilla. Pour dry ingredients into a large bowl and combine with a spatula. Stir in chocolate chips.
4. Refrigerate for at least 30 minutes.
5. Roll or scoop dough into 12 large balls (about 2 Tbsp each), spread out over 2 baking sheets.
6. Bake for 14-16 minutes. Allow cookies to cool and enjoy!

Mix It Up:

Make these chocolate cookies, monster cookies by adding your favorite nuts/candies, or just leave them plain! Top with flaky sea salt for a fancy presentation and salty flavor!

Difficulty: 🧁🧁
Yields: 24 Cookies

Ingredients:

- ⅔ cup cold butter, cubed into small pieces
- 1 cup granulated sugar
- Zest of 1 lemon
- 2 Tbsp lemon juice
- 1 large egg
- 1 tsp vanilla
- 1 tsp baking powder
- ½ tsp salt
- 2 cups all purpose flour
- 1 Tbsp milk

Lemon glaze:

- 1 cup powdered sugar
- 2 Tbsp lemon juice

LEMON SUGAR COOKIES

Directions:

1. Cream the butter and sugar with an electric mixer. Add lemon juice, zest, vanilla, milk, and eggs.
2. In a small bowl, whisk together flour, baking soda, and salt.
3. Slowly mix dry ingredients with wet ingredients until dough forms.
4. Cover and let it chill in the fridge for 1-2 hours.
5. Preheat the oven to 350° and line or grease 2 baking sheets.
6. Roll into golf-ball sized mounds and place on baking sheets.
7. Bake for 12-14 minutes. Allow to cool completely.
8. While cookies cool, prepare the glaze by whisking powdered sugar with lemon juice.
9. Dip each cookie in the glaze, and let the glaze harden.

Mix It Up:

Make your own glaze by adding different flavors such as pureed raspberries or strawberries! Fancy up your presentation by sprinkling sugar on the cookies, and top with fresh fruit! Use these cookies to make an ice cream sandwich on a summer day!

COOKIE DOUGH HUMMUS

Ingredients:

- 1 can drained and rinsed chickpeas/garbanzo beans
- ⅔ cup packed brown sugar
- 2 tsp vanilla extract
- 1/4 cup peanut butter
- 1/4 cup chocolate chips
- 3 Tbsp oat flour
- 2 Tbsp milk
- 1 Tbsp maple syrup (optional)

Directions:

1. Pulse oats in a food processor/blender to make an oat flour.
2. Add the rest of the ingredients into a food processor with the blended oats (except the chocolate chips), blend until smooth.
3. Stir in chocolate chips.

Mix It Up:

Switch out the chocolate chips for some m&ms. Try adding some spice with cinnamon, or add your favorite chopped nuts for extra crunch! Dip with strawberries, graham crackers, pretzels, or just eat it plain with a spoon!

Difficulty: 🧁 🧁
Yields: 24 Cookies

Ingredients:

- ¾ cup granulated sugar
- ¼ cup brown sugar
- ¼ tsp baking soda
- 6 tbsp softened butter
- ½ cup chocolate chips
- 3 tbsp cacao powder
- 1 cup flour
- ¼ tsp salt
- 1 tsp vanilla
- 2 eggs

FUDGY CHOCOLATE COOKIES

Directions:

1. Preheat the oven to 350°. Line or grease 2 baking sheets.
2. Melt butter and chocolate chips together and set aside to cool.
3. Beat eggs, brown sugar, granulated sugar, and vanilla with an electric mixer for 3-5 minutes.
4. Add melted butter and chocolate and stir with a spatula.
5. Stir in flour, salt, baking powder, and cacao powder.
6. Cover and refrigerate for 1 hour.
7. Use a small spoon or cookie scoop to form the dough into 24 balls and place on baking sheets.
8. Bake for 10 minutes, and cool for 10 minutes.

Mix It Up:

Make these fudgy cookies into an ice cream sandwich or frost with your favorite frosting such as cream cheese or berry frosting! You can add a few mini marshmallows into each cookie for a warm gooey flavor or top with flaky sea salt to balance out the sweetness!

UNICORN SUGAR COOKIES

Ingredients:

- ⅔ cup cold butter, cubed into small pieces.
- 2 cups all purpose flour
- 1 egg
- 1 cup granulated sugar
- 1 tsp vanilla
- 1 tsp baking powder
- ½ tsp salt
- 1 Tbsp milk
- Food coloring

Directions:

1. With an electric mixer, cream butter and sugar. Add in egg, vanilla, and milk.
2. In a separate bowl whisk flour, salt, and baking powder.
3. Pour half of the flour mixture into the wet ingredients and mix. Add the other half of flour and mix until it turns into dough.
4. Split dough up into 3-5 different sections and dye each section a different color.
5. Cover dough and refrigerate for 1-2 hours.
6. Preheat the oven to 375°.
7. Roll out dough and make different designs using your colored dough!
8. Bake for 10-12 minutes.

Mix It Up:

This colorful dough is like playdough! Use it to create whatever shapes and designs you like! Spiral the dough together, or simply roll it all up into balls to create a "tie-dye" cookie!

Difficulty: 🧁🧁
Yields: 12 Cupcakes

Ingredients:

Cupcakes:
- 2 large eggs
- 1 cup sugar
- ⅔ cups cup softened butter
- 1 tsp vanilla extract
- 1 ½ cup all purpose flour
- 1 tsp baking powder
- ½ baking soda
- ¼ tsp salt
- ½ cup milk

Frosting:
- 1 cup softened butter
- 3 cups powdered sugar
- 1 tsp vanilla
- Pinch of salt
- Food coloring (optional)

SUPER SIMPLE VANILLA CUPCAKES

Directions:
1. Preheat the oven to 350°, and line a muffin tin with cupcake liners.
2. Cream butter and sugar together with an electric mixer. Add eggs and vanilla extract.
3. In a separate bowl whisk flour, baking powder, baking soda, and salt
4. Slowly pour flour mixture into wet ingredients, rotating between a little bit of flour and milk, stir with a spatula until fully combined.
5. Divide batter into 12 muffin tins.

Mix It Up:
Experiment with different frosting flavors by adding cream cheese, cacao powder, or fruit preserves! You can add sprinkles to the batter for a funfetti cupcake, or hollow out the center of the cupcake and fill it with a jam or sprinkles for a tasty surprise when you bite into the cupcake!

Ingredients:

Frosting:
- ½ cup softened butter
- 2 tablespoons milk
- 1 ½ cup powdered sugar
- 1 teaspoon vanilla extract

Cake Pop:
- 12 vanilla Cupcakes (warm and fresh, because the steam helps bind the cake pop)
- 4 cups Candy/chocolate melts
- Sprinkles/toppings
- Skewers/cake pop sticks

CAKE POPS

Directions:
1. Prepare the frosting, using an electric mixer, beat butter, milk, powdered sugar, and vanilla for 3-5 minutes.
2. In a large bowl, break up the cupcakes until fully mashed, and stir in frosting
3. Roll the mashed cupcakes and frosting into small balls (1 tablespoon each- golf ball sized). Place on a greased baking sheet and refrigerate for 1 hour.
4. Melt candy melts in the microwave or stove top.
5. Dip the tip of a skewer into candy melts and stick cake pop onto it, only push the stick about half way through the cake pop
6. Dip and fully coat each cake pop in candy melts
7. Sprinkle with your toppings of choice
8. Return to the refrigerator for 10 minutes or until the candy coating hardens.

Mix It Up:
Decorate your cake pops with colorful toppings. If you are making these for a special occasion or holiday use special toppings such as crushed candy canes, drizzled chocolate, crumbled oreos, fruity pebbles, whatever you want!

Notes:
You can use leftover pre-frosted cupcakes for this recipe. However, since they would be room temperature and not fresh, throw all of the cupcakes with frosting into a bowl and mash them together. Then proceed with the regular steps, 3-8

Difficulty: 🧁
Yields: 10 Balls
Gluten Free, Dairy Free

Ingredients:

- 1 cup of dates
- 1 cup of nuts (Walnuts or Pecans work best)
- 1 tsp of vanilla
- 1 Tbsp cacao powder
- 1 Tbsp of peanut Butter
- ⅓ cup rice crispy cereal (optional)

DATE BALLS

Directions:

1. Put all ingredients into a food processor, except for rice crispy cereal.
2. When the mixture has formed a dough-like consistency, add rice crispy cereal and roll into balls.
3. Let them chill in the refrigerator for 20 minutes.

Mix It Up:

For a little bit more crunch, add some chopped nuts after blended. For a different flavor try adding coconut flakes or a little bit of maple syrup!

Ingredients:

- 1 cup creamy peanut butter
- 1 cup chocolate chips
- 1 tsp vegetable oil
- 6-8 cups chex cereal
- 1 ½ - 2 cups powdered sugar

PUPPY CHOW/ MUDDY BUDDIES

Directions:

1. Melt peanut butter, vegetable oil, and chocolate in a saucepan over the stove, or pop in the microwave for 30 second intervals until melted.
2. Pour melted chocolate and peanut butter over Chex cereal in a Ziploc bag, or a bowl with a lid, and shake until all the chex is coated in the chocolate sauce.
3. Refrigerate for a few minutes, or until room temperature, but not completely hardened.
4. Pour in powdered sugar as desired, and shake to combine.

Mix It Up:

Try making a "birthday" flavored puppy chow by replacing the chocolate with white chocolate, use half of the peanut butter, and add sprinkles! Warning: despite its name, this chocolaty treat is not for puppies!!

Ingredients:

- 3 Tbsp of honey
- 3/4 cups of oats
- 1 Tbsp of vanilla
- 1/4 cup of chocolate chips
- 1/4 cup of Peanut Butter
- 1/4 cup of coconut flakes

PEANUT BUTTER BALLS

Directions:

1. Mix the honey, vanilla, and peanut butter together in a small bowl.
2. Stir in oats and coconut flakes.
3. Once combined, add chocolate chips.
4. Roll into bite-sized balls, and refrigerate for 20 minutes.

Mix It Up:

Try adding your own mix-ins such as a tiny bit of nutella, 1 tsp of hot cocoa powder, chia seeds or a different nut butter!

Ingredients:

- 3 egg whites, room temperature
- ⅓ cup granulated sugar
- 1 tsp vanilla
- 4 cups shredded coconut
- ½ cup melted chocolate (optional)

COCONUT MACAROONS

Directions:

1. Preheat the oven to 325°. Line or grease a baking sheet.
2. Whip egg whites until thick and foamy.
3. Add vanilla extract and sugar.
4. Fold in coconut shreds.
5. Use a cookie scoop to form the mixture into balls on a baking sheet. The coconut mixture is not very doughy and tends to fall apart, so I highly recommend using a cookie/ice cream scoop to form it into balls.
6. Bake for 10 minutes or until light brown.
7. Once cooled, dip or drizzle with chocolate, if using.

Mix It Up:

Use your imagination to decorate these little coconut cookies. You could use food coloring to brighten them up! To make these similar to an Almond Joy candy, top each macaroon with one almond and coat in chocolate.

CHOCOLATE PEANUT BUTTER CUPS

Ingredients:

- ⅔ cup creamy peanut butter
- 2 Tbsp butter
- 2 Tbsp brown sugar
- 1/2 cup powdered sugar
- 10 oz melted chocolate (about 2 cups)

Directions:

1. Line a mini muffin tin, or grease it with cooking spray/butter.
2. In a small pot, over medium heat, stir the butter, peanut butter, and brown sugar until melted.
3. Cover and refrigerate until cool.
4. Melt half of the chocolate.
5. Pour 1-2 teaspoons of melted chocolate in each muffin cup. Refrigerate for 20 minutes to harden.
6. Roll peanut butter mixture into marble size balls, and flatten into a small disc. Place 1 peanut butter circle over each chocolate base.
7. Melt the remaining chocolate. Cover all of the peanut butter with the rest of the chocolate.

Mix It Up:

Play around with sizes and different types of chocolate! You can also try to make these with caramel (recipe on page 24).

Difficulty: 🧁🧁
Yields: 24 bites

Ingredients:

- ¼ cup brown sugar
- 10 graham crackers
- ½ cup melted butter
- 2 bars chocolate
- 12 large marshmallows (halved)

S'MORES BITES

Directions:

1. Preheat the oven to 350°, and prepare a mini muffin tin by greasing with cooking spray or butter.
2. In a large ziploc bag, mash the graham crackers until it turns into a crumbly flour.
3. Combine mashed graham cracker with melted butter and brown sugar.
4. Separate into the muffin tin about a tablespoon for each cup and press it into a shallow bowl.
5. Bake for 8-10 minutes.
6. Cut your marshmallows in half, and separate the chocolate into 24 small pieces.
7. Place one piece of chocolate and one marshmallow half in each graham cracker bowl.
8. Turn the oven on broil and let it bake for about 2 minutes, be sure to keep an eye on it to not let you marshmallows burn!
9. Cool for 20 minutes

Mix It Up:

Change up the flavors with special marshmallows, such as cinnamon or peppermint marshmallows for a holiday treat! Try replacing the regular chocolate with your favorite chocolate such as a piece of a Reese's peanut butter cup or a piece of a Heath bar!

Ingredients:

- ¼ cup butter
- ¼ cup sweetened condensed milk
- ¼ cup brown sugar
- ¼ tsp salt (and more to sprinkle on top)
- ¼ cup light corn syrup
- ½ tsp vanilla

SOFT AND CHEWY CARAMELS (MICROWAVE:):

Directions:

1. Grease or line an 8x4 container.
2. Place butter in a microwave safe bowl and melt.
3. Add condensed milk, both sugars, corn syrup, and salt.
4. Microwave for 1:30 seconds and then stir it.
5. Return it to the microwave for another 1:30 seconds.
6. Stir it and add the vanilla extract.
7. Pour into your prepared container and let it chill in the fridge for 1 hour.
8. Slice and sprinkle with salt!

Mix It Up:

These easy chewy caramels can be a great gift during the holiday seasons so feel free to dress them up with your own creativity by dipping/ drizzling them in chocolate! You could even add cinnamon for a warm cozy flavor! For some texture, top with your favorite chopped nuts or chocolate chips!

Difficulty:   
Yields: 36 macarons
Gluten Free

Ingredients:

Macaron shell:

- 1 ½ cup almond flour
- 1 cup confectioners sugar
- 3 egg whites (room temperature)
- ¼ tsp lemon juice
- 1 tsp vanilla
- ½ cup granulated sugar
- Food Coloring (if desired)

Whipped berry butter filling:

- ½ cup jam
- 2 Tbsp confectioners sugar
- ½ cup softened butter
- 1 tsp lemon juice

FRENCH MACARONS

Directions:

1. Preheat the oven to 300°. Line or grease 2 baking sheets.
2. Sift almond flour and confectioners, blend in a food processor for 30 seconds.
3. Whip egg whites in a clean bowl with an electric mixer until foamy. Add the lemon juice, and very slowly add the granulated sugar, a tiny bit at a time. When your egg whites form soft peaks, add the food coloring and the vanilla. Continue mixing until it forms stiff peaks. (This is when you lift up the whisk and the egg whites stand up).
4. Gently fold in the dry ingredients in 3 parts. The final mixture should be able to slowly fall off your spatula in a thick band without breaking (undermixed) nor falling fast and runny (overmixed). With a piping bag, pipe the macaron batter in 1 inch circles onto the baking sheets. Tap each baking sheet 10 times on the counter to rid your macaron shells of bubbles. Let sit for 10 minutes.
5. Bake Macarons for 14 minutes. As they cool, prepare the filling. Beat your butter until creamy with an electric mixer. Pour in the rest of your ingredients and mix until well combined. Spread the filling onto half of the cooled macaron shells, using the other half as tops.

There are unlimited flavors of macarons, and as you practice, macaron-making will become much easier. Use your imagination for new flavors, by dyeing the shell new colors, and playing around with new fillings such as buttercream, or a jelly filling.

Difficulty: 🧁🧁
Yields: 8 servings

Ingredients:

- 6 cups blueberries (fresh or frozen)
- 2 Tbsp sugar
- 3 Tbsp flour

Topping:

- ½ cup flour
- 2 ½ cup oats
- ½ tsp cinnamon
- 1 cup brown sugar
- ½ cup almonds (optional)
- ½ cup softened butter

BLUEBERRY CRISP

Directions:

1. Preheat the oven to 375°. Grease or line a 13x9 inch pan.
2. In a large bowl stir flour, sugar and blueberries.
3. Transfer blueberries to the prepared pan.
4. Mix flour, oats, brown sugar, cinnamon, almonds (if desired), and butter.
5. Fully cover the blueberries with oat mixture.
6. Bake for 35-40 minutes.

Mix It Up:

Blueberry crisp is a delicious fruity treat that doesn't have to be reserved just for blueberries. Mix it up with some strawberries, peaches, or your favorite berry! For a summery flavor spritz, add 1 tsp of lemon juice to the blueberries.

Difficulty: 🧁🧁
Yields: 15 rice crispy treats
Gluten Free

Ingredients:

- 12 cup rice crispy cereal
- 8 cups mini marshmallows
- 10 Tbsp salted butter
- ½ tsp salt

BROWN BUTTER RICE CRISPY TREATS

Directions:

1. In a large pot melt the butter. Continue to let it cook on medium heat while stirring until light brown specks appear.
2. Add marshmallows and salt and stir until melted.
3. Stir in cereal until fully coated with melted marshmallows.
4. Spread onto a greased baking sheet and flatten with clean hands .
5. Cool completely and enjoy!

Mix It Up:

Though rice krispies are delicious, they are not very colorful. Think of these gooey treats as a blank canvas for your imagination! Dress them up with some sprinkles, or dip them in colorful candy melts! Make your rice crispy treats extra special by using a different cereal such as fruit loops, coco puffs, or cheerios! You can even use cookie cutters, or a knife to shape your treats.

Difficulty: 
Yields: 8 squares

Ingredients:

Crust:

- 12 graham crackers- 1 ½ cup
- 6 Tbsp melted butter
- ¼ cup packed brown sugar

Filling:

- 4 egg yolks
- Zest of 2 limes (2 tsp, and more if desired for topping)
- ½ cup lime juice
- 2 tbsp cream cheese
- 1 14 oz can sweetened condensed milk

Whipped Cream Topping:

- 2 Tbsp cream cheese
- ¼ cup powdered sugar
- 1 cup heavy whipping cream

KEY LIME PIE BARS

Directions:

1. Preheat the oven to 350°. Line an 8x8 inch pan with parchment paper, with some hanging over the edges for easy removal.
2. In a large ziploc bag, mash graham crackers with a spoon or rolling pin.
3. In a small bowl, stir graham cracker crumbs, melted butter, and brown sugar.
   Press into the pan. Bake the crust for 10 minutes.
4. Prepare the filling by beating cream cheese and egg yolks. Add sweetened condensed milk, lime juice, and zest.
5. Pour filling over cooled graham crust and bake for 18-20 minutes.
6. While it cools, prepare the topping by whipping heavy cream until it forms stiff peaks. Add powdered sugar and cream cheese.
7. Spread topping onto cooled key lime pie. Sprinkle lime zest on top, if desired.
   Refrigerate for 1-2 hours. Slice and serve.

Experiment with the presentation of your key lime pie bars, use a piping tip to create a whip cream design. You could also try adding your favorite berries. And as always, adjust to your liking. For more citrus, add extra lime zest!

Difficulty: 🧁 🧁
Yields: 8 Bars
Gluten Free

Ingredients:

- 1 cup rice krispies
- 1 cup oats
- ½ cup corn flakes
- 1 cup peanut butter
- ⅓ cup honey
- ¼ cup brown sugar
- ½ tsp vanilla
- Pinch of salt
- ¼ cup chocolate chips

GRANOLA BARS

Directions:

1. Preheat the oven to 350°.
2. Line an 8x8 inch pan with parchment paper.
3. Toast the oats in the oven for 10 minutes.
4. In a medium pot heat the peanut butter, honey, brown sugar, salt, and vanilla, stirring until combined.
5. Pour oats, rice krispies, corn flakes, and chocolate chips into the pot and combine.
6. Press mixture into the pan and refrigerate for at least 1 hour.

Mix It Up:

Feel free to make these an extra sweet treat with your favorite mix-ins such as dried fruit, chopped nuts, mini marshmallows, m&ms, or peanut butter chips. Try making double chocolate granola bars by drizzling/dipping them in melted chocolate and adding 1 Tbsp of cacao powder with the oats.

Difficulty: 🧁 🧁
Yields: 8 Bars

Ingredients:

- ½ cup brown sugar
- ¼ cup water
- 6 peaches, sliced
- ¼ tsp cinnamon
- 3/4 cup sugar
- 5 tablespoons melted butter
- 1 cup flour
- 1 ⅓ teaspoons baking soda
- ⅔ cup milk
- ½ teaspoon salt

PEACH COBBLER

Directions:

1. Preheat the oven 350°and grease a 13x9 inch pan.
2. In a medium pot, cook the peach slices, brown sugar, and water on the stove over medium heat.
3. Pour peaches into the pan and spread them out to fully cover the bottom.
4. In a separate bowl, whisk the cinnamon, sugar, flour, baking soda, and salt.
5. In a small bowl whisk together melted butter and milk.
6. Pour milk and butter into dry ingredients and stir until combined.
7. Dollop spoonfuls of the batter over the peaches. Using a spatula, spread the batter out to cover most of the peaches.

Mix It Up:

Use your favorite sliced fruits instead of peaches, such as apples! For a nutty aroma and extra buttery flavor, brown the butter instead of just melting it.

Difficulty: 🧁
Yields: 4 Pops
Gluten Free

Ingredients:

- 2 Tbsp for peanut butter
- ½ cups for chocolate chips
- 2 bananas (halved)
- Skewers or popsicle sticks
- Toppings (sprinkles, nuts, etc.)

MONKEY POPS

Directions:

1. Stick the skewers into the bananas.
2. Melt the chocolate chips and peanut butter together in the microwave or stovetop.
3. Fully dip each banana in the melted chocolate mixture.
4. Sprinkle bananas with your favorite toppings.
5. Place chocolate covered bananas on a plate and refrigerate for 10 minutes, or until hard.

Mix It Up:

These monkey pops are delicious and very customizable! Make different flavors for each pop, by using different chocolates; white, dark, or milk! Play around with toppings, cinnamon, m&ms, marshmallows, fruity pebbles whatever your sweet tooth craves!

Difficulty:
Yields: 4 Popsicles
Gluten Free

Ingredients:

- ¼ cup packed brown sugar
- 1 tablespoon cornstarch
- Pinch of salt
- ¼ cup cocoa powder
- 1 cup milk
- ¼ cup semi-sweet chocolate
- Popsicle molds

FUDGESICLES

Directions:

1. In a small bowl whisk cacao powder, brown sugar, cornstarch, and salt.
2. In a small pot combine dry ingredients and milk over the stove on medium heat, stirring constantly.
3. When thick and creamy, turn off heat and stir in chocolate until melted.
4. Once cooled, pour into 4 popsicle molds and freeze for 4 hours or overnight.

Mix It Up:

After frozen, you can dip your popsicles in melted chocolate for a crisp chocolate layer. Or you can add your favorite chopped berries into the chocolate mixture before you put them in the freezer for some fruity flavor!

Difficulty:
Yields: 4 Cups
Gluten Free, Dairy Free

Ingredients:

- 4 cups cubed frozen watermelon (frozen for at least 4 hours)
- 2 Tbsp of sugar
- 2 Tbsp lime juice
- ½ tsp salt

WATERMELON SLUSHIE

Directions:

1. Toss all ingredients into a blender and blend just until smooth.
2. Serve right away, so it doesn't melt!

Mix It Up:

This refreshing summer treat is delicious topped with mint leaves. Add a few different frozen fruits, such as oranges, pineapples, or peaches, to create your own flavor! If you add other fruits, use a 4:1 ratio between the watermons and the other fruits, because the frozen liquid in watermelons gives this drink its slushy consistency. For a thinner smoothie-like consistency, continue to blend, and add 1 cup of ice.

Difficulty: 
Yields: 4 Cups
Gluten Free, Dairy Free

Ingredients:

- 4 cups water
- 3/4 cup lemon juice (about 4 lemons)

Simple syrup:

- ½ cup sugar
- ¼ cup water
- 15-20 mint leaves

MINT LEMONADE

Directions:

1. Heat ¼ cup water on the stove, when it starts to bubble, add sugar and stir until it dissolves.
2. Allow water and sugar to simmer for 3 minutes.
3. Add mint leaves, turn off the heat, and set aside to cool.
4. Combine lemon juice and water
5. Once the mint simple syrup has cooled, strain into a container.
6. Combine simple syrup with lemon juice and water.
7. Serve over ice, and top with fresh mint leaves!

Mix It Up:

Make this "pink" lemonade, with some food coloring, or add different juices. Try making your own soda, with sparkling water instead of 4 cups of regular water.

Difficulty: 🧁
Yields: 2 Cups
Gluten Free

Ingredients:

- 2 cup vanilla ice cream
- 1 cup frozen strawberries
- ½ cup cream cheese
- ½ cup milk

STRAWBERRY CHEESECAKE MILKSHAKE

Directions:

1. Combine all ingredients in a blender and blend until smooth.
2. Pour into 2 cups and enjoy!

Mix It Up:

Add your favorite toppings, such as fresh strawberries, or whipped cream! Play around with different ice cream flavors and topping to create your own special milkshake.

Difficulty: 🧁 🧁
Yields: 12- 14 crepes

Ingredients:

- 1 ½ cups flour
- 1-2 Tbsp sugar
- 4 eggs
- 2 cups milk
- 3 Tbsp melted butter

CLASSIC CREPES

Directions:

1. Whisk all ingredients together in a bowl.
2. Heat a small saucepan, greased with butter, on the stove, on medium/low setting.
3. Pour about 1/4 cup of batter onto the pan at a time and cook on both sides for about 1 minute.
4. Fill with desired toppings and bon appetit!

Mix It Up:

This recipe is great to learn about ratios, as you can modify to your liking and it will still taste delicious. For more flavor add a pinch of salt to your crepe batter. Fill your crepe with savory flavors such as ham, cheese, pesto, or veggies. Or spread nutella, jams, and whipped cream for a sweeter crepe!

Difficulty: 🧁

Yields: 1 baking sheet of yogurt bark

Ingredients:

- 2 1/2 cups plain yogurt
- 2 Tbsp fruit jelly/jam
- 2 Tbsp honey
- 1/2 cup granola
- 1 cup fresh berries

YOGURT BARK

Directions:

1. Combine in yogurt, honey and jam in a bowl.
2. Pour yogurt onto a parchment paper lined baking sheet.
3. Top with berries and granola.
4. Freeze for 3 hours or overnight.
5. Break the bark into pieces and store in an air-tight container in the freezer.

Mix It Up:

Instead of using plain yogurt and jam, try this recipe with fruit-flavored or vanilla yogurt. Play around with your favorite toppings such as coconut flakes, nuts, or drizzled honey!

Difficulty: 🧁🧁

Yields: 4-6 (varies depending on size of waffle iron)

Ingredients:

- 1 cup flour
- 2 Tbsp sugar
- 1 tsp baking powder
- 2 eggs
- 1 cup milk
- ¼ cup oil
- 1 tsp vanilla

FLUFFY WAFFLES

Directions:

1. In a large bowl, whisk dry ingredients, flour, sugar, and baking powder.
2. In a separate bowl, whisk wet ingredients (except for the eggs) milk, oil, and vanilla, until just combined.
3. Separate the eggs, combine egg yolks with wet ingredients, and place egg whites in a small bowl, set aside.
4. Using an electric mixer, in the small bowl, whip egg whites until fluffy.
5. Using a spatula, pour wet ingredients into dry ingredients, and slowly mix. Pour in whipped egg whites, and stir carefully, just until combined. Be sure not to overmix!
6. Heat up the waffle machine and pour about ¼ cup batter on it.

Mix It Up:

Try adding some chocolate chips into the batter and top with nutella for a chocolate lover! Or make a fruity waffle by adding fresh berries to the batter and top with homemade strawberry butter, (recipe on page 35). Decorate your waffles with whipped cream, powdered sugar, or any of your favorite toppings

Difficulty: 🧁
Yields: 1 Cup
Gluten Free

Ingredients:

- ½ cup softened butter
- ½ cup strawberries, quartered (about 8 small strawberries)
- 1 Tbsp honey
- 2 Tbsp powdered sugar
- pinch salt

STRAWBERRY BUTTER

Directions:

1. Toss all ingredients into blender
2. Blend until smooth and fluffy.
3. Store in the refrigerator in an airtight container.

Mix It Up:

You can not mess up this strawberry butter, so make it according to your taste preference! If you would like it sweeter add another tablespoon of honey! Or youn can try making your own butter recipe with a different berry!

Difficulty: 🧁 🧁
Yields: 12 muffins

Ingredients:

- 1 ½ cup quick oats
- 1 cup milk
- ½ cup packed brown sugar
- ½ greek yogurt
- 2 eggs
- 1 tsp vanilla extract
- ½ cup all purpose flour
- 1 tsp baking powder
- ½ tsp baking soda
- ½ tsp salt
- 1 cup blueberries (fresh or frozen)

BLUEBERRY OATMEAL POWER MUFFINS

Directions:

1. Preheat the oven to 400° and grease a muffin tin or line with cupcake liners.
2. In a blender or food processor, blend oats for a few seconds until oats are broken into small pieces, but not quite a smooth flour.
3. In a small bowl soak oats in milk, set aside for 30 minutes.
4. In a large bowl combine brown sugar, yogurt, eggs, and vanilla.
5. In a third bowl, whisk flour, salt, baking powder, and baking soda.
6. Using a spatula, fold soaked oats into wet ingredients. Once combined, slowly add dry ingredients and fold in blueberries.
7. Pour batter into the muffin tin and bake for 22-24 minutes. Cool for 10 minutes.

Mix It Up:

These Blueberry muffins taste like oatmeal in a muffin! I love to sprinkle cinnamon and sugar over my oatmeal, so whether you like honey or fresh berries, feel free to top these power muffins however you like your oatmeal!

Difficulty: 🧁 🧁

Yields: 24 donut holes

Ingredients:

- 1 ½ cup flour
- 2 tsp baking powder
- 1 tsp of salt
- 5 tbsp butter
- ½ cup packed brown sugar
- 1 egg
- 1 tsp vanilla
- 1 banana
- 1/2 cup milk

Topping:

- ½ cup granulated sugar
- 2 Tbsp cinnamon
- 6 Tbsp butter

BANANA "DONUT" MUFFINS

Directions:

1. Preheat the oven to 350° and grease a small muffin tin.
2. In a large bowl, mash banana, and whisk with melted butter, egg, brown sugar, milk, and vanilla.
3. Add flour, baking soda, and salt, mix with a spatula.
4. Using a cookie scoop, so the top is rounded, distribute batter into muffin tin.
5. Bake for 10-12 minutes.
6. In a small bowl whisk cinnamon and granulated sugar. In a second small bowl, melt the butter.
7. Once cooled, roll each mini muffin in melted butter then in the cinnamon and sugar.

Mix It Up:

These muffins are inspired by donut holes, so you can coat them in a chocolate or vanilla glaze instead of cinnamon and sugar if you'd like! For extra cozy flavors, add your favorite spices to the batter such as 1/4 tsp of cinnamon or nutmeg.

www.ingramcontent.com/pod-product-compliance
Lightning Source LLC
Chambersburg PA
CBHW042049110726
48006CB00002B/348